PRINCEWILL LAGANG

Beyond the Search Bar: The Sergey Brin Chronicles

First published by PRINCEWILL LAGANG 2023

Copyright © 2023 by Princewill Lagang

All rights reserved. No part of this publication may be reproduced, stored or transmitted in any form or by any means, electronic, mechanical, photocopying, recording, scanning, or otherwise without written permission from the publisher. It is illegal to copy this book, post it to a website, or distribute it by any other means without permission.

Princewill Lagang asserts the moral right to be identified as the author of this work.

First edition

This book was professionally typeset on Reedsy.
Find out more at reedsy.com

Contents

1. Introduction — 1
2. In the Shadow of Silicon Valley — 2
3. Code and Collaboration — 4
4. The Google Revolution — 6
5. Navigating New Frontiers — 8
6. Turbulence and Transformation — 10
7. Innovations and Impact — 12
8. Paradigm Shifts and Reflections — 14
9. Legacy and Future Horizons — 16
10. The Ever-Evolving Narrative — 18
11. The Uncharted Frontiers — 20
12. Reflections on a Journey — 22
13. Beyond the Horizon — 24
14. Summary — 26

1

Introduction

The introduction sets the stage for "Beyond the Search Bar: The Sergey Brin Chronicles," offering a glimpse into the dynamic world of technology and the transformative impact of one of its pioneers, Sergey Brin. It provides a brief overview of Brin's early life, his journey from Russia to Stanford, and the formation of Google. The introduction establishes the narrative's focus on the evolution of Google, Brin's visionary leadership, and the ethical considerations accompanying technological advancements. It serves as an enticing entry point, inviting readers into the intricate tapestry of innovation, challenges, and societal impact that unfolds in the subsequent chapters.

2

In the Shadow of Silicon Valley

The air in Moscow was crisp as Sergey Brin strolled through the courtyard of the prestigious Stanford University in the heart of Silicon Valley. It was the late 1990s, and the promise of the internet was beginning to permeate every aspect of life. Sergey, a young computer science graduate student from Russia, was on a journey that would change the digital landscape forever.

The chapter opens with a vivid description of the Stanford University campus, setting the stage for Sergey Brin's early days in the United States. The Silicon Valley atmosphere is introduced, emphasizing the vibrant and innovative energy that defined the region during the dot-com boom.

As Sergey walks through the courtyard, the narrative delves into his background, tracing his roots from Russia to the United States. Sergey's passion for computer science and his relentless pursuit of knowledge become evident. The reader is given a glimpse into his early life, the challenges he faced, and the dreams that fueled his ambition.

The chapter explores Sergey's initial encounters with the world of technology at Stanford. His interactions with professors, fellow students, and the burgeoning internet community shape his perspective and ignite his curiosity. The reader witnesses the birth of ideas and the formation of friendships that would later play pivotal roles in the creation of one of the most influential companies in the world.

The atmosphere of Silicon Valley is further painted through scenes of bustling coffee shops, late-night coding sessions, and the hum of excitement that permeates the air. The chapter introduces key figures who would eventually collaborate with Sergey, building the foundation for the journey ahead.

As the narrative progresses, there's a foreshadowing of the challenges and opportunities that lay beyond the horizon. The dot-com boom and the frenzied pace of technological advancement set the backdrop for Sergey's exploration of what lies "Beyond the Search Bar."

The chapter concludes with Sergey Brin standing at the threshold of a new era, both in his life and in the world of technology. The reader is left with a sense of anticipation, eager to accompany Sergey on his journey beyond the familiar confines of academia and into the uncharted territories of innovation.

Through meticulous storytelling and a focus on the human aspects of Sergey Brin's early experiences, the chapter sets the stage for a compelling exploration of the man behind the search engine giant and the era that shaped him.

3

Code and Collaboration

As Sergey Brin dove deeper into the world of computer science at Stanford, the chapter opens with the infectious buzz of collaboration and creativity within the university's computer labs. Sergey, fueled by an insatiable curiosity, begins to forge alliances with like-minded individuals who share his passion for pushing the boundaries of technology.

The narrative explores the dynamic relationships that emerge between Sergey and other key players in the early days of what would become Google. Introducing Larry Page, another brilliant mind with a fervor for innovation, the chapter chronicles the serendipitous meeting that would alter the course of internet history. The synergy between Sergey and Larry becomes palpable as they embark on joint projects, laying the groundwork for what would eventually become one of the most iconic partnerships in the tech world.

Amidst the lines of code and the late-night brainstorming sessions, the chapter delves into the challenges faced by Sergey and Larry as they navigate the intricate landscape of turning ideas into reality. The reader witnesses the birth pangs of what would become the Google search engine, with glimpses into the algorithmic complexities and the determination that propelled them forward.

The chapter not only focuses on the technical aspects but also delves into the human side of the story. Sergey's relationships with other students, mentors, and industry influencers contribute to the mosaic of influences that shape the trajectory of Google. The reader gains insight into the culture of innovation and the camaraderie that defined the early days of the company.

As the narrative unfolds, the chapter explores the pivotal decision to transform their project into a business venture. Sergey and Larry navigate the intricacies of entrepreneurship, from securing funding to making strategic decisions that would define the future of Google. The reader is taken behind the scenes, witnessing the blend of idealism and pragmatism that characterized their approach to building a company that would go on to redefine the digital landscape.

The chapter concludes with a sense of accomplishment and anticipation. Sergey Brin, alongside Larry Page and their growing team, stands at the threshold of a new era. The reader is left with a sense of the collaborative spirit that fueled the creation of Google, setting the stage for the global impact it would soon have and the challenges that lay ahead in the next chapter of "Beyond the Search Bar: The Sergey Brin Chronicles."

4

The Google Revolution

The chapter opens against the backdrop of the late 1990s and the dawn of the new millennium. Sergey Brin and Larry Page, armed with their innovative search engine technology, embark on the journey to revolutionize the way information is accessed and organized on the internet. The narrative unfolds as Google transitions from a promising startup to a global tech powerhouse.

The reader is taken through the challenges and triumphs of scaling Google's infrastructure to meet the demands of an ever-expanding user base. The chapter delves into the development of groundbreaking algorithms, such as PageRank, which played a pivotal role in reshaping the landscape of online search. Sergey's relentless pursuit of refining search capabilities becomes a driving force behind Google's ascent to prominence.

As Google gains traction, the chapter explores the company's early attempts to monetize its services and the introduction of AdWords—a groundbreaking advertising platform that would later become a cornerstone of Google's revenue model. The reader witnesses the delicate balance between maintaining user experience and generating income, a challenge that would shape Google's business strategy for years to come.

The narrative also touches upon the cultural ethos fostered within Google, emphasizing Sergey Brin's commitment to creating a workplace that values creativity, innovation, and a sense of purpose. The chapter introduces key figures who contributed to Google's success and explores the unique corporate culture that set the company apart in the tech industry.

Amidst the company's meteoric rise, the chapter doesn't shy away from the controversies and ethical dilemmas that accompany such rapid growth. Google's increasing influence sparks debates about privacy, data collection, and the ethical responsibilities of a technology giant. Sergey Brin grapples with the complexities of balancing innovation with ethical considerations, setting the stage for the evolving narrative of Google's impact on society.

The chapter concludes with Google firmly established as the go-to search engine for users worldwide. Sergey Brin, now recognized as a visionary in the tech industry, faces new challenges and opportunities on the horizon. The reader is left with a sense of the transformative power of Google's revolution and a foreshadowing of the chapters yet to unfold in "Beyond the Search Bar: The Sergey Brin Chronicles."

5

Navigating New Frontiers

As the digital landscape evolves, so does Sergey Brin's journey in "Beyond the Search Bar." Chapter 4 opens with Google at the forefront of the tech industry, but the narrative quickly shifts to the challenges and innovations that lie ahead for Sergey and his team.

The chapter explores Google's expansion beyond search. Sergey, driven by an insatiable curiosity, leads initiatives into new frontiers, from the development of innovative products to ambitious projects that stretch the boundaries of technology. The reader witnesses the birth of products like Google Maps, Google Earth, and the foray into mobile operating systems, showcasing Sergey's commitment to making information universally accessible and useful.

The narrative also delves into the complexities of managing a rapidly growing and diversifying company. Sergey grapples with the balance between maintaining the company's innovative spirit and the operational challenges of a tech giant. The chapter introduces the intricacies of leadership and decision-making as Google transforms into a multifaceted technology conglomerate.

The rise of Google as a global force is accompanied by increased scrutiny. The chapter explores the regulatory challenges and controversies that arise as Google's influence extends into various facets of daily life. Sergey Brin finds himself navigating the delicate dance between innovation and responsibility, facing public scrutiny and regulatory inquiries.

The reader is immersed in the dynamic tech landscape of the early 21st century, witnessing the emergence of competitors, strategic partnerships, and the continuous evolution of Google's product portfolio. Sergey's visionary leadership style is further revealed as he steers the company through uncharted territory, embracing risks and learning from setbacks.

Amidst the technological advancements, the chapter delves into Sergey Brin's personal journey, exploring his philanthropic efforts and interests beyond the tech realm. The reader gains insights into the man behind the tech mogul, understanding Sergey's commitment to making a positive impact on the world.

As the chapter draws to a close, the reader is left with a sense of anticipation, eager to discover what lies ahead for Sergey Brin and Google. The evolving narrative hints at the challenges and opportunities that will shape the next phase of "Beyond the Search Bar: The Sergey Brin Chronicles."

6

Turbulence and Transformation

As "Beyond the Search Bar" progresses, Chapter 5 delves into a period of turbulence and transformation in the life of Sergey Brin and the Google empire. The narrative unfolds against the backdrop of a rapidly changing technological landscape, marked by new challenges, controversies, and the relentless pursuit of innovation.

The chapter begins with Google facing increased scrutiny on various fronts, from antitrust concerns to debates over user privacy. Sergey Brin finds himself in the midst of regulatory inquiries and public debates, grappling with the ethical dimensions of Google's influence on information and its impact on society. The reader witnesses Sergey's introspective moments and the internal struggles that come with balancing corporate growth and societal responsibility.

In the face of these challenges, the narrative explores Google's response to the changing dynamics of the tech industry. Sergey spearheads initiatives to address privacy concerns, enhance user control, and navigate the intricate web of legal and regulatory frameworks. The chapter sheds light on the complexities of managing a global technology giant under the watchful eyes of regulators and the public.

Amidst the turbulence, the chapter also highlights Google's continued commitment to technological innovation. Sergey Brin leads the company through the development of groundbreaking projects, from advancements in artificial intelligence to ventures into healthcare technology. The reader gains insights into Sergey's enduring belief in the transformative power of technology to improve lives.

As Google undergoes internal restructuring and strategic shifts, the narrative explores Sergey Brin's role in shaping the company's future. The reader witnesses the evolution of Google into Alphabet Inc., a conglomerate encompassing a diverse range of ventures beyond the realm of search. Sergey's strategic vision and adaptability come to the forefront as Google navigates the complexities of maintaining innovation while diversifying its portfolio.

The chapter also provides glimpses into Sergey's personal life, exploring how the challenges and transformations within Google impact his worldview and priorities. The reader witnesses the intersection of personal and professional growth in the life of Sergey Brin, offering a more comprehensive understanding of the man behind the technological revolution.

As Chapter 5 concludes, the narrative leaves the reader on the edge of anticipation, eager to uncover the next phase of Sergey Brin's journey and the ongoing saga of "Beyond the Search Bar." The chapter sets the stage for the continued evolution of Google and the ever-changing landscape of technology and society.

7

Innovations and Impact

As "Beyond the Search Bar" enters its next chapter, the narrative unfolds against a backdrop of continued innovation, societal impact, and personal evolution in Sergey Brin's journey. Chapter 6 explores Google's forays into groundbreaking technologies and the enduring influence of Sergey's vision on the ever-expanding digital frontier.

The chapter opens with Google's ventures into emerging technologies, such as artificial intelligence, machine learning, and quantum computing. Sergey Brin's fascination with pushing the boundaries of what is possible is evident as the narrative takes the reader through the development of cutting-edge projects. From self-driving cars to advancements in natural language processing, the chapter showcases Google's commitment to staying at the forefront of technological innovation.

The reader is invited to witness the societal impact of Google's projects and the ethical considerations that accompany such transformative technologies. Sergey grapples with questions of responsibility, transparency, and the potential implications of Google's innovations on privacy, security, and social dynamics. The chapter delves into the delicate balance between progress and ethical considerations, revealing the moral compass that guides Sergey's decisions.

Amidst the technological advancements, the narrative also explores Google's efforts in addressing global challenges. Sergey Brin's philanthropic initiatives and the impact of Google.org on issues such as education, healthcare, and environmental sustainability come to the forefront. The chapter provides a glimpse into Sergey's commitment to leveraging technology for the betterment of society, showcasing a holistic perspective beyond the confines of corporate success.

As Google's influence continues to expand, the chapter sheds light on the evolving role of Sergey Brin within the company and the broader technological landscape. The reader witnesses the complexities of leadership and the strategic decisions that shape Google's trajectory, from strategic partnerships to acquisitions that further solidify Google's position in the tech industry.

The narrative also delves into Sergey's personal growth and reflections on the impact of technology on society. The chapter explores his evolving perspectives on the responsibilities of technology leaders, the challenges of navigating the public eye, and the ongoing quest for a balance between innovation and ethical considerations.

Chapter 6 concludes with a sense of both accomplishment and anticipation. The reader is left with a comprehensive view of Google's innovations, societal impact, and the personal and professional evolution of Sergey Brin. As the story moves forward, the reader is poised to explore the next chapters of "Beyond the Search Bar" and the unfolding legacy of Sergey Brin in the ever-changing landscape of technology and humanity.

8

Paradigm Shifts and Reflections

As "Beyond the Search Bar" progresses into its seventh chapter, the narrative unfolds against the backdrop of paradigm shifts in the tech industry, global events, and the ongoing evolution of Sergey Brin's journey. Chapter 7 delves into transformative moments, reflective insights, and the continued impact of Google and its co-founder.

The chapter opens with the tech industry undergoing seismic changes. The reader is immersed in the era of artificial intelligence, virtual reality, and the internet of things. Sergey Brin, driven by an unwavering commitment to staying at the forefront of innovation, leads Google through these technological shifts. The narrative explores Google's ventures into new territories, from cutting-edge AI applications to ambitious projects that redefine human-computer interaction.

As Google continues to shape the digital landscape, the chapter delves into the evolving dynamics of the company. Sergey Brin's role in Alphabet Inc. and the strategic decisions that shape the conglomerate's portfolio of companies come to the forefront. The reader witnesses the intricate balance of managing a diverse range of ventures under the umbrella of Alphabet, showcasing

Sergey's adaptability and strategic vision.

The narrative also explores the impact of global events on Google and its co-founder. From geopolitical challenges to societal shifts, the chapter navigates the complex intersections between technology, politics, and culture. Sergey's reflections on the responsibilities of tech leaders in an increasingly interconnected world provide a nuanced perspective on the role of technology in shaping society.

Amidst these transformations, the chapter delves into Sergey Brin's personal journey. The reader gains insights into his experiences, challenges, and moments of introspection. The narrative explores how personal growth, family life, and the ever-changing tech landscape intersect, offering a more intimate portrayal of Sergey Brin beyond his public persona.

As the chapter progresses, the reader witnesses Google's continued efforts in addressing ethical considerations, privacy concerns, and the societal impact of its technologies. Sergey's commitment to transparency, accountability, and responsible innovation becomes a central theme, showcasing a continued dedication to the ethical dimensions of technology.

Chapter 7 concludes with a sense of reflection and anticipation. The reader is left with a panoramic view of the transformative moments, challenges, and ongoing evolution in the life of Sergey Brin and the Google empire. As the narrative propels forward, the reader is poised to uncover the next chapter in "Beyond the Search Bar" and the continued legacy of Sergey Brin in the ever-evolving landscape of technology and humanity.

9

Legacy and Future Horizons

As "Beyond the Search Bar" reaches its eighth chapter, the narrative navigates through the culmination of Sergey Brin's journey, the lasting legacy of Google, and the future horizons that lie ahead. Chapter 8 encapsulates the profound impact of Google on the digital landscape and society, reflecting on Sergey Brin's contributions and the ongoing evolution of technology.

The chapter opens with a retrospective lens, highlighting the transformative influence of Google on information accessibility, communication, and the very fabric of modern life. Sergey Brin's visionary leadership and commitment to innovation are celebrated as the narrative weaves through the milestones, challenges, and societal shifts that defined Google's legacy.

The reader is immersed in the myriad ways in which Google's products and services have become integral to daily life. From search and advertising to cloud computing and artificial intelligence, the chapter explores how Sergey's relentless pursuit of excellence shaped Google into a global technology giant with a far-reaching impact.

The narrative delves into the company's continued efforts in addressing ethical considerations, privacy concerns, and the responsible deployment of technology. Sergey's reflections on the ethical responsibilities of tech leaders provide insights into the evolving mindset within the industry and the ongoing quest for a harmonious integration of technology into society.

As the narrative unfolds, the chapter explores Sergey Brin's transition from day-to-day operations to a more strategic and advisory role. The reader witnesses how his influence extends beyond Google, encompassing philanthropic initiatives, mentorship, and a commitment to nurturing the next generation of innovators.

The future horizons come into focus as the chapter explores emerging technologies, societal trends, and the evolving role of technology in shaping the world. Sergey's thoughts on the future of innovation, the potential of technology to address global challenges, and the responsibilities of the tech industry provide a forward-looking perspective.

Chapter 8 concludes with a sense of fulfillment and continuation. The reader is left with a panoramic view of Sergey Brin's journey, the enduring legacy of Google, and the ever-expanding frontiers of technology. As "Beyond the Search Bar" reaches its conclusion, the narrative invites the reader to reflect on the profound impact of Sergey Brin's contributions and the ongoing narrative of innovation in the dynamic intersection of technology and humanity.

10

The Ever-Evolving Narrative

In the concluding chapter of "Beyond the Search Bar," the narrative continues to unfold, embracing the ever-evolving nature of technology, society, and the legacy of Sergey Brin. Chapter 9 invites the reader to reflect on the dynamic intersections of innovation, ethics, and the ongoing narrative that transcends the confines of a single individual or company.

The chapter opens with a glimpse into the contemporary tech landscape, where new players, disruptive technologies, and societal shifts redefine the parameters of what is possible. Sergey Brin's legacy is examined against this backdrop, emphasizing the enduring impact of his vision on the trajectory of the tech industry.

As the narrative weaves through the latest developments in technology, the reader is prompted to contemplate the ethical considerations that accompany these advancements. The chapter explores how the tech industry, influenced by the lessons of the past, strives to navigate the complexities of privacy, accountability, and responsible innovation.

The reader is taken on a journey through the ongoing evolution of Google and its offshoots under Alphabet Inc. The chapter delves into the company's response to contemporary challenges, the strategic decisions shaping its future, and the embodiment of Sergey's vision in the initiatives undertaken by the next generation of leaders.

Beyond the corporate realm, the narrative expands to explore the broader implications of technology on society. Sergey Brin's philanthropic efforts, the impact of Google.org, and the ongoing commitment to addressing global challenges provide a lens through which the reader can appreciate the multifaceted influence of technology on humanity.

The chapter concludes with a contemplation of the future horizons. The reader is prompted to envision the possibilities and potential pitfalls that lie ahead, considering the role of technology in shaping the human experience. Sergey Brin's journey serves as a testament to the dynamic interplay between innovation, responsibility, and the ever-expanding narrative of progress.

In the closing pages of "Beyond the Search Bar," the reader is left with a sense of continuity and the understanding that the story is not static. As the tech industry, society, and individuals continue to evolve, the legacy of Sergey Brin becomes a part of a larger narrative—an ongoing exploration of the interdependence between humanity and the technologies that shape our world. The reader is encouraged to embrace the fluidity of this narrative, acknowledging that the quest for knowledge, innovation, and ethical considerations will persist beyond the confines of these pages.

11

The Uncharted Frontiers

In this final chapter, the narrative of "Beyond the Search Bar" takes a leap into the uncharted frontiers of the future. Chapter 10 serves as an epilogue, offering reflections on the ever-evolving legacy of Sergey Brin and the ongoing saga of technology in the 21st century.

The chapter opens with a contemplation of the contemporary technological landscape, shaped by the innovations, challenges, and societal shifts of the preceding chapters. The reader is invited to peer into the latest advancements, disruptive technologies, and emerging trends that define the current state of the tech industry.

As the narrative navigates through the complexities of the present, the lasting impact of Sergey Brin's journey is celebrated. The chapter explores how his vision, commitment to innovation, and ethical considerations continue to resonate in the ethos of the tech industry. The reader is prompted to consider the enduring influence of individuals like Sergey Brin on the trajectory of technology and society.

Beyond the individual, the narrative widens its scope to encompass the collective efforts of the tech community. The chapter delves into collaborative initiatives, ethical frameworks, and the evolving role of technology in addressing global challenges. The reader is encouraged to explore the collaborative spirit that propels humanity forward in the pursuit of knowledge and progress.

The epilogue also considers the responsibilities of future leaders and technologists. The narrative contemplates the ethical considerations, the importance of transparency, and the imperative of fostering a tech landscape that benefits humanity at large. The reader is prompted to envision the role they might play in shaping the narrative of technology in the years to come.

As the chapter draws to a close, the reader is left with a sense of continuity and the acknowledgment that the story does not end here. The uncharted frontiers of the future beckon, and the narrative of "Beyond the Search Bar" serves as a testament to the perpetual exploration, adaptation, and innovation that characterize the human-technology symbiosis.

In the final pages, the reader is encouraged to embrace the unfolding narrative, recognizing that the journey into the future is a shared endeavor. The legacy of Sergey Brin becomes a part of this larger tapestry—a reminder that the quest for knowledge, innovation, and responsible technology will persist as humanity navigates the uncharted frontiers that lie ahead.

12

Reflections on a Journey

In this reflective chapter, "Beyond the Search Bar" takes a pause to delve into the retrospective insights and personal reflections that emerge from the journey chronicled in the preceding chapters. Chapter 11 serves as a space for contemplation, where the reader is invited to consider the themes, lessons, and the resonance of Sergey Brin's story in the broader context of technology and human progress.

The chapter opens with a revisit to key moments, pivotal decisions, and transformative periods in Sergey Brin's life and the evolution of Google. The reader is prompted to reflect on the impact of these moments, both on an individual level and in shaping the trajectory of the tech industry.

As the narrative weaves through the tapestry of innovation, challenges, and societal shifts, the chapter delves into the enduring themes that emerged from Sergey Brin's journey. Themes of curiosity, resilience, ethical considerations, and the interplay between technology and humanity are explored, providing the reader with a framework for deeper reflection.

The reader is encouraged to consider the resonance of Sergey Brin's story in the context of their own experiences and the evolving nature of technology in their lives. The narrative becomes a mirror, reflecting the shared quest for knowledge, the pursuit of innovation, and the ethical responsibilities that accompany technological advancements.

In this chapter of introspection, the narrative also explores the broader implications of technology on society. The reader is prompted to contemplate the role of individuals, corporations, and the collective global community in shaping a future where technology aligns with human values and contributes to the betterment of the world.

The chapter concludes with an invitation to envision the possibilities and responsibilities that lie ahead. The reader is encouraged to carry forward the spirit of inquiry, the commitment to ethical considerations, and the understanding that the narrative of technology is an ongoing, collaborative endeavor.

As the pages turn, and the reader reaches the conclusion of this reflective chapter, they are left with a sense of resonance and a deeper understanding of the themes woven into "Beyond the Search Bar." The journey, both of Sergey Brin and the reader, becomes a testament to the shared exploration of the intersection between technology and humanity—an exploration that continues beyond the confines of this narrative.

13

Beyond the Horizon

In this final chapter of "Beyond the Search Bar," the narrative extends its gaze beyond the immediate horizon, contemplating the limitless possibilities and challenges that lie ahead. Chapter 12 serves as a culmination of the journey, an exploration of what the future may hold for technology, society, and the ongoing legacy of Sergey Brin.

The chapter opens with a survey of the contemporary technological landscape, acknowledging the rapid pace of innovation, emerging technologies, and the dynamic shifts that shape the present. The reader is prompted to consider the trajectory of the tech industry, reflecting on how the lessons from the past can inform future endeavors.

As the narrative peers into the future, the chapter delves into the potential trajectories of technology. It explores the impact of artificial intelligence, advancements in biotechnology, and the continued evolution of the digital realm. The reader is encouraged to envision the ways in which these technologies might shape the human experience and influence the societal landscape.

Ethical considerations take center stage as the chapter contemplates the responsibilities of individuals, corporations, and the global community in steering the course of technology. The reader is prompted to reflect on the importance of ethical frameworks, transparency, and a collective commitment to ensuring that technology serves the well-being of humanity.

The narrative also considers the ongoing legacy of Sergey Brin. The reader is invited to reflect on the enduring influence of his vision, the impact of Google, and the broader implications for the tech industry. The chapter explores how individuals inspired by Sergey's journey might contribute to the continued narrative of innovation, responsibility, and progress.

Amidst the contemplation of the future, the chapter acknowledges the uncertainties and challenges that may arise. The narrative becomes a call to action, encouraging the reader to actively participate in shaping the trajectory of technology, advocating for ethical practices, and contributing to a future where innovation aligns with human values.

As "Beyond the Search Bar" draws to a close, the reader is left with a sense of empowerment—an understanding that the journey into the future is a collective endeavor. The narrative becomes a torchbearer, lighting the way for those who seek to navigate the uncharted territories of technology with curiosity, responsibility, and a commitment to the betterment of humanity.

14

Summary

"Beyond the Search Bar" is a comprehensive narrative that chronicles the life and impact of Sergey Brin, co-founder of Google. The story unfolds across twelve chapters, each offering a detailed exploration of key moments, challenges, and innovations in Brin's journey and the evolution of the tech giant. From his early days at Stanford to the creation of Google and its transformation into Alphabet Inc., the narrative captures the dynamic landscape of the tech industry. The chapters delve into the ethical considerations, societal impacts, and personal reflections that accompany technological advancements. As the narrative progresses, it extends beyond Brin's individual story to reflect on the broader implications of technology on society, urging readers to consider the ethical responsibilities and possibilities that lie ahead. The epilogue serves as a reflective space, encouraging contemplation on the enduring legacy of Sergey Brin and the ongoing narrative of technology and human progress. The final chapter looks to the future, envisioning the limitless possibilities and challenges that technology may bring, and inspiring readers to actively shape the trajectory of innovation for the betterment of humanity.

www.ingramcontent.com/pod-product-compliance
Lightning Source LLC
LaVergne TN
LVHW010444070526
838199LV00066B/6187